Banner Designs

for the

Church Year

Banner Designs

for the

Church Year

JANE DEBORD
and LINDA ISBELL

CONCORDIA PUBLISHING HOUSE · SAINT LOUIS

This edition published 2006
Copyright © 1984, 2006 Concordia Publishing House
3558 S. Jefferson Avenue
St. Louis, MO 63118-3968
www.cph.org • 1-800-325-3040

Originally published under the title *Banner Designs for Celebrating Christians*
© 1984 Concordia Publishing House.

Written by Jane DeBord and Linda Isbell

Scripture quotations, unless otherwise indicated, are taken from the The Holy Bible, English
Standard Version, copyright © 2001 by Crossway Bibles, a division of Good News Publishers.
Used by permission. All rights reserved.

Scripture quotations marked RSV are from the Revised Standard Version of the Bible,
copyright 1952, © 1971 by the Division of Christian Education of the National Council
of the Churches of Christ in the United States of America. Used by permission.
All rights reserved.

Scripture quotations marked KJV are from the King James or Authorized Version of the Bible.

Manufactured in the United States of America

1 2 3 4 5 6 7 8 9 10   15 14 13 12 11 10 09 08 07 06

Contents

Getting Started

This book comes with everything you need to get started making banners for your church. It covers a broad spectrum of subjects and festivals in the church year to provide you with the right banner design. You can take the tools in this book and use them as they are, or you can tailor the banner patterns to suit your taste or circumstances. Change the colors or fabrics to fit the setting and your budget. Add some tabs or trim to fit the theme. It can be as easy or complicated as you wish.

Be creative.

      Have fun.

            And raise your banners to God's glory.

Place and Purpose of Banner

Before you choose a location for your banner, remember that placement determines the size and also influences the potential effect of the banner. If the chosen setting is a formal sanctuary, keep in mind the mood or atmosphere that already exists—the architecture, stained glass, crosses, and the colors of existing paraments, carpeting, and curtains.

Look around your church. Use banners wherever they can accomplish their purpose. A banner not only can enhance the beauty of its surroundings, but it can also motivate, inspire, and call forth responses of action or thought. A banner can be the perfect way to call attention to a specific concern of the church (for example: stewardship campaign). Let your banner work for you!

Scale to Size

Every banner design in this book can be easily scaled to a size suitable for your particular space. All methods involve using roll art paper or butcher paper, which comes in a variety of widths. If a wide roll is not available to get a large enough sheet on which to draw the banner pattern, simply tape smaller pieces together. Several methods can be used to obtain the required banner size:

1. If an opaque projector is available, enlarge the design in the book to the desired size and trace it onto paper. This is by far the easiest method.

2. If an opaque projector is not available another easy method is to use an overhead transparency projector. Make a copy of the banner to a sheet of acetate transparency film. Use the film and the projector to enlarge the design to the size desired and trace it onto paper.

3. If you don't have access to projectors, enlarge the banner design according to a scale. Each design is measured in inches (for example: 3" × 5½"). The scale for enlarging the design is to have one inch represent one foot (1 inch equals 1 foot—a 3" × 5½" design becomes a 3' × 5½' banner). Make a copy of the banner you wish to enlarge. Draw a grid on the chosen banner design with horizontal lines across at every inch and vertical lines down at every inch. Draw the outside perimeter of the finished banner size (for example: 3' × 5½') on the roll art paper. Draw a grid on the paper at every foot in the same manner. The lines of the banner design in the book will cross the grid at certain points. These points should be marked on the design and then transferred to the large pattern at the corresponding points. Lines are then drawn to connect the points by copying the curve or angle from the design in the book. The design may vary slightly from the original but should be similar enough to accomplish the intended purpose.

If the space where the banner will hang does not allow you to enlarge it according to the scale of one inch to one foot, or if you choose to make the banner larger than the intended scale, you can create your own scale. (For example a 1" = 1 1/2' scale will mean that a 3" × 5½" design will make a 4½' × 8¼' banner. A 1" = ½' scale will produce a 1½' × 2¾' banner). The same system of drawing grids on the design and the pattern, transferring the points, and drawing the approximate lines can then be used.

4. For smaller banners you can use a photocopier to enlarge the pattern.

Estimating Fabric Needs

For the background fabric, add at least 4" to the length and width. Include extra material for any tabs or edges you intend to incorporate. Using the overall pattern, measure the individual pieces to determine how much of each fabric to buy. Remember to allow for error and experimentation. These measurements will also determine the amount of fusible webbing to purchase if you decide to use it, but add at least 12" for test samples. Most fabrics come in 45" widths so plan accordingly. Note: If the fabric has a nap, add more yardage to allow nap of the pieces to match.

Yardage Chart

Inches	Yards
4.5	1/8
9	1/4
18	1/2
22.5	5/8
27	3/4
31.5	7/8
36	1

Know Your Colors and Textures

Colors can visually express emotion. For example, red, yellow, and their derivatives reflect joy and high moments, whereas the cooler tones of blue and its variations suggest contemplation or tranquility. The use of colors will determine the emphasis of each banner. For instance, using complementary colors such as violet and yellow against each other produces a striking, jump-out-at-you effect, while using monochromatic colors will result in a more subdued effect.

An analogous combination, a graduation of progressive tones of similar colors, such as yellow, orange, orange-red, red, produces an effect of increasing intensity. This technique works well when a powerful effect is desired.

A triadic combination consists of three colors that are equidistant on the color wheel, which usually creates a lighter, exciting look. To aid you in your choices a color wheel is provided.

The church also has a tradition of symbolic meanings for color:

RED
- Day of Pentecost, Reformation, Palm Sunday, Maundy Thursday;
- symbolizes Holy Spirit, love, royalty, sin, sacrifice, fire, loyalty

GREEN
- seasons of Pentecost and Epiphany;
- symbolizes growth, fruitfulness, abundance, victory, hope

VIOLET
- Lent, Advent, Palm Sunday, Ash Wednesday;
- symbolizes humility, repentance, royalty, solemnity, sorrow, grief

BLACK
- Good Friday, Ash Wednesday;
- symbolizes sin, death, sorrow, absence, evil

WHITE
- Christmas, Easter, Transfiguration of Our Lord, Epiphany, Trinity Sunday, All Saints' Day, Maundy Thursday, Thanksgiving, New Year;
- symbolizes purity, truth, innocence, holiness, redemption, faith, light

BLUE
- Advent;
- symbolizes hope, heaven, truth, beginnings, love, faithfulness, tranquility

YELLOW OR GOLD
- Easter;
- symbolizes royalty, blessings, marriage

Textures reflect moods as much as colors do. For example, marriage is a festive occasion calling for the finest of fabrics. A funeral, on the other hand, combines grief and celebration. The banner reflects this through a combination of rough and high sheen textures.

The seasons of Lent and Advent call for some rough-textured fabrics, symbolizing in Lent the agony and suffering of our Lord and in Advent His humble birth in a crude manger. High sheen fabrics are suitable for most other seasons and occasions.

Color Wheel

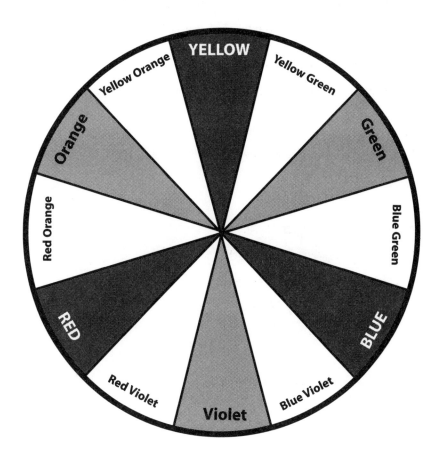

Choosing Fabric

There are many fabrics available, but cotton and cotton blends work best. Felt is by far the easiest to work with, as you do not need to line it and it does not shrink or fray. Avoid stretchy knits, 100% polyester fabrics, and loose weaves.

At the store, arrange the fabrics and trim you've chosen next to each other and stand as far away as possible to see how well the colors combine. Keep switching until you have exactly what you want.

Most of the fabrics listed below come in a variety of colors and are reasonably priced. Try your local fabric store for the best selection, but don't forget sale and remnant tables for great bargains.

LIGHT WEIGHT	MEDIUM WEIGHT	HEAVY WEIGHT
Muslin	Satin	Cotton duck
Skimmer muslin	Chino	Heavy felt
Chintz	Trigger Cloth	Heavy duck
Metallic fabrics	Broadcloth	Denim
Organdy	Flannel	Poplin plus
Sateen	Poplin	
Taffeta	Twill	
China silk	Corduroy	
	Linen-look fabric	
	Gabardine	
	Upholstery	
	Drapery	

A Note about Cutting Fabrics

Woven fabrics have a grain—threads that run lengthwise and crosswise. Threads that run lengthwise do not stretch. Threads that run crosswise often do stretch.

It is very important to cut and sew banner background fabric and lining *with* the grain so the finished banner hangs evenly and straight. Cutting fabric against the grain results in a banner that twists and puckers when it is assembled and that hangs awkwardly when it is finished. No amount of stretching, pinning, or sewing will correct the wrinkles, puckers, and ridges that result when the straight of grain is not followed. (Felt does not have a grain.)

Making the Banner

1. After you have chosen a banner design, use the suggested colors and materials, or decide alternate colors and fabrics appropriate for the theme.

2. Draw the banner pattern to scale. Keep this pattern in one piece to use as a guide for the placement of individual pieces.

3. Decide how much fabric is needed for each part of the banner. Purchase the fabric, lining (same yardage as for the background piece), rods, glue or thread, and fusible interfacing. For the background piece purchase six inches more than the finished banner size to allow for top and bottom finishing. If thin or light fabric will be covering dark fabric at any spot, you will need to use double fabric and glue or fusible interfacing so the darker fabric will not show through.

4. If possible, preshrink fabrics and washable fusible interfacing to prevent puckering. Afterward, iron the fabric so it is wrinkle free. Do not iron the fusible interfacing.

5. Trace each piece of the pattern. Be certain before this step is done that you have studied the banner to see if any part of a particular piece is covered by another piece. For example, the words "Wonderful, Counselor" in the banner "He Shall Be Called..." cover part of the starburst in the background. The entire piece must be traced, including lines that are covered by another part of the banner.

6. Number the pattern pieces in the order in which they will be placed on the background, layer by layer. For example, on the "He Shall Be Called..." banner the starburst would be number 1 and the letters that go on top of the starburst would be number 2.

7. Cut the background. Be sure you have left at least six inches to finish the top and bottom of the banner. Cut the pattern pieces.

8. There are two easy ways to assemble the banner. Depending on the fabric you choose, you can use fabric glue or fusible interfacing. The easiest method is to glue the pieces together. All-purpose glue, craft glue, rubber cement and glue guns are all readily available. Check your local fabric store for other options. You can use a thick tacky craft glue to reduce the shrinkage and bleeding of most fabrics. Test your glue on a few scraps first to see which works best with your fabrics and choose the most economical. Note that fabric glue does not bond with polyester fabrics.

   If you prefer to use fusible interfacing, lay out the fusible interfacing on the bottom, then the fabric, and then the pattern piece on top. Pin all three pieces together. Cut the pieces. Caution: If you have two pattern pieces that are adjacent, be sure to cut one at least ¼" larger than the pattern calls for so one piece is slightly under the other, not butted together. This makes stitching easier; you will have to stitch only the top piece where two pieces come together. For example, on the "Let Earth Receive Her King" banner the garments of the people are adjacent. One should be cut to fit under the other; they should not be butted together.

9. Place all pieces on the background to be certain there is enough room for spacing.

10. Remove all pieces except for the first layer. Glue each piece layer by layer, or iron on the pieces layer by layer, following the directions that come with the fusible interfacing. Iron all pieces with fusible interfacing before you begin stitching, as this produces a more even effect than stitching layer by layer.

11. If desired, stitch the banner. For a finished look and durability, use a zigzag stitch to outline the various portions of the banner. A straight stitch may be used, but it will produce a more informal look. Adjust the zigzag stitch according to the finish desired. A closer stitch will produce a more definite outline; a more open stitch will hold the pieces in place but will not create the outline effect.

12. You are ready to line your banner!

Lining

When you have assembled the banner, determine the exact finished length you desire it to be. The sides and bottom will be stitched with a ⅝" seam. If the top is to have a rod inserted through it, add 3½" to the finished length of the banner, trimming away any excess at the top and bottom. It is important that all edges be very straight so the banner will hang evenly.

Next, lay the lining fabric on a cutting board or flat surface. Place the banner on top of the lining with the wrong side up. Carefully pin the two together at the sides, top, and bottom so banner and lining do not shift. Cut the lining to the same size as the banner. Stitch only the sides and bottom together with a ⅝" seam, leaving the top open as on a pillowcase.

Trim the seams, clip the corners, and turn the banner right side out. Press it, using a damp cloth. Open it out at a side seam, right side up. Turn the seam toward the lining, and stitch as close to the seam as possible, being careful not to catch the front of the banner in the seam.

Repeat for the bottom and the other side. (You will not be able to stitch all the way to the bottom because of the corner.) This is known as the Bishop Method; it holds the lining in place and prevents the edge of the lining from rolling to the front.

Turn the top raw edge of the banner and lining under ½", stitch, and press firmly. Then turn the top under to create a 3½" hem. Pin and press firmly in place. Stitch 3" from the top of the banner to form the hem. This will create a 3-inch casing for insertion of a rod.

If tabs are to be used in place of a casing for hanging the banner, these should be attached to the back of the banner. Pin in place, edge stitch the tabs, then stitch again ¼" from the first stitching. Be certain the tabs all measure the same length from the top of the banner so the banner will hang evenly.

Finishing Touches

The addition of decorative tabs, borders, and other types of trim to the finished banner can enhance its beauty and add to the impact of its message. These finishing touches are drawn into most of the designs or are suggested along with the banner. Use the suggested finishing touches or create your own from these categories:

1. *Borders*. Borders are optional but can add contrast if you find the banner blends into the wall. You can use ribbon or other trim. Rubber stamps and fabric inkpads are particularly effective for creating a repeated border pattern. Choose one of the design's colors or complementary colors for the best effect.

2. *Tabs*. Banners can be hung by inserting a rod through a casing at the top of the banner or through tabs sewn across the top. If tabs are chosen, the color should be the same color and material as the background fabric.

If you would like to have tabs at the top of a banner, the width of the banner determines the number of loops needed to support its weight and prevent sagging. Make sure the tabs and the spaces between them are approximately the same width. There are several ways to make tabs. You can cut them from the background fabric and fold them over, or you can sew or glue on separate pieces. If you would like to add tabs to the bottom of a banner, use the methods just described or simply cut them out along the bottom edge. These tabs do not require a rod.

3. *Hangers*. The rod used to hang the banner should be chosen to accommodate the weight of the banner and to complement the style and theme. First, a rod must be able to hold the banner securely. Then consider the types of rods available and choose

one that fits the fabric and theme of the banner. A wooden rod is best with banners that have rough textures or simple fabric; a brass rod is more suitable for banners with dressy or formal materials.

4. *Edges.* The bottom of the banner can be much more than a straight line. Points, arches, or other indentations or alterations can add dimension to the banner or focus attention on certain of its elements. Tassels, fringe, macramé, or other trim can be also attached to the bottom.

5. *Trim.* The bottom of the banner can be functional as well as decorative. Many of the banners include suggestions for trim. When possible, the trim should emphasize the message of the banner. For example, NIKA across the bottom of "No Greater Love" enforces the belief that Christ was victorious over death. Here are several possibilities, but use your imagination to come up with your own innovative ideas:

Camel bells	Brass bells
Christmas ornaments	Seashells
Musical instruments	Crosses
Crowns	Doves
Nails	Flowers
Butterflies	Keys
Greek letters	Triangles
Fish	Old jewelry
Macramé symbols	Coins
Stitched and stuffed items such as hearts or circles	Ribbon, rickrack, sequins, beads, or buttons
Stained or colored glass pieces	Plastic, wood, or metal geometric shapes

Banner Designs

Prepare Him Room

A voice cries: "In the wilderness prepare the way of the LORD; make straight in the desert a highway for our God."

Isaiah 40:3

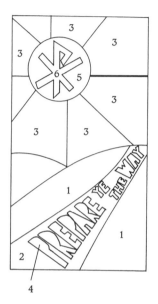

Suggested Colors

1–Bright green
2–Bright yellow
3–Dark turquoise
4–Magenta
5–Royal purple
6–White

Symbolism and Meaning

As the voice of the prophet Isaiah echoes across the centuries, "Prepare the way of the Lord," we hear the call to prepare our hearts for the coming of Christ. Although the road that lies before each of us may present entanglements and obstacles that block our efforts and divert our energies at every step, we still hear the clear call to prepare a way for Him. This season of the year has its share of entanglements and obstacles to divert our minds from Him, but as we fix our gaze on the straight path toward the great light shining on the horizon, bearing the Greek letters for His name, chi (X) and rho (P), we are reminded of the One who has already prepared the way for us, the Light of the world, the Christ.

Suggested Materials

Use medium to heavy weight fabric in purple for the background and magenta for the letters. Use medium weight fabric such as chino for the star, hillsides, and path with the star in dark turquoise. Use heavy white fabric such as chino or heavy satin for Chi-Rho.

Suggested Titles

Prepare Him Room
Prepare Ye the Way
Prepare the Way of the Lord

Lift up your heads, O gates! And be lifted up, O ancient doors, that the King of glory may come in.
Psalm 24:7

Let Earth Receive Her King

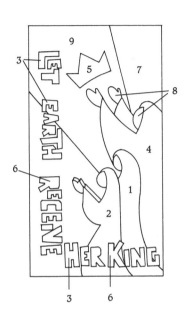

Suggested Colors

1–Bright green	6–Red
2–Dark turquoise	7–Royal purple
3–Green	8–Tan
4–Light purple	9–Yellow
5–Magenta	

Symbolism and Meaning

The yellow ray of light beams continuously from heaven, symbolizing Christ's steadiness and readiness to enter our lives. The worshipers, God's people, open their hearts and reach toward the Lifegiver, signifying their willingness to receive Him as King. The crown represents the kingly role of Christ and Lord of our lives. "Let Earth Receive Her King," a lyric from the favorite Christmas carol, "Joy to the World," inspires the message of this banner.

Suggested Materials

Use taffeta or other shiny material for the ray of light. All other fabrics can be medium to heavy weight with a variety of textures.

Suggested Titles

Receive Your King
Let Earth Receive Her King

He Shall Be Called . . .

For unto us a child is born, unto us a Son is given, and the government shall be upon His shoulder, and His name shall be called "Wonderful, Counselor, The mighty God, The everlasting Father, The Prince of Peace." **Isaiah 9:6 KJV**

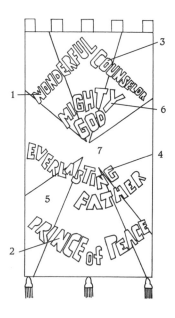

Suggested Colors

1–Dark turquoise

2–Fuchsia

3–Gold

4–Green

5–Light violet

6–Red

7–Royal purple

Symbolism and Meaning

The prophets of old repeatedly foretold the coming of the promised hope of Israel, the long-awaited Messiah. Speaking through Isaiah the prophet, God promised to save His people through the birth of a child who would personify the character of God Himself, becoming to the people a Wonderful, Counselor, a Mighty God, an Everlasting Father, a Prince of Peace.

The background in this banner symbolizes the jubilant sound of the trumpet of the ages heralding the birth of hope for humankind. One can almost hear the joyful strains of Handel's Messiah reverberating the many names that describe the King, the Child, the Savior who was to come.

Suggested Materials

Use medium weight, shiny fabrics in vivid colors such as satin, chino, or quiana for the letters. Use medium weight fabric such as chino or broadcloth in light violet for the background and the royal purple starburst. Add shimmery tassels for trim on the bottom.

And the Word became flesh and dwelt among us, and we have seen His glory, glory as of the only Son from the Father, full of grace and truth.
John 1:14

Behold His Glory

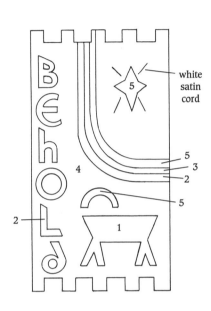

white satin cord

Suggested Colors
1–Camel

2–Gold

3–Red

4–Royal purple

5–White

Symbolism and Meaning
The Christmas story tells us that God acted. To a darkened world, symbolized by the dark royal purple background, He sent a Light that the darkness could not overcome. In this banner we see symbolically the result of His love and His desire for harmony with His creation.

The tricolored ray emanating earthward from heaven represents three aspects of Christ's nature: gold for His divinity, red for His humanity, and white for His righteousness.

The four-pointed star and the manger with nimbus illustrate the reality of His action, the birth of His Son, Jesus Christ.

The simple word "Behold" expresses our response of awe to God's gift of love.

Suggested Materials
Use medium weight shiny fabrics such as satin and chino for the star, tricolored ray, and nimbus; coarse medium weight upholstery-type fabric for the manger; and gold lamé for the letters. Accent the star with white satin cord as indicated.

Suggested Titles
Behold His Glory

Behold

Glory to God in the Highest

Glory to God in the highest, and on earth peace among those with whom He is pleased! **Luke 2:14**

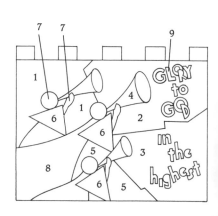

Suggested Colors

1–Bright royal blue	6–Silver
2–Dark purple	7–Tan
3–Dark turquoise	8–White
4–Gold	9–Yellow
5–Navy blue	

Symbolism and Meaning

The same gladness that seized the shepherds on the hillsides of Judea that first Christmas night is rekindled within us each year. The good news of Christ's birth stirs wonder and amazement anew at the completeness of God's love for His children despite our unworthiness.

The trumpets of the heavenly hosts shatter the stillness of the night, as indicated by the broken lines of the background sky. They proclaim the glad tidings of Christ's birth while inspiring praise and glory to God.

Suggested Materials

Background fabrics should be medium to heavy weight broadcloth, chino, or upholstery. The angels' gowns are white chino or other shiny fabric. Their heads are shiny yellow chino or taffeta, and their hands are tan medium weight fabric. The trumpets are gold lamé. The angels' wings are silver lamé. The letters are yellow chino or another shiny material. Trumpet ornaments would be attractive trim for the bottom of the banner.

Suggested Titles

Glory to God in the Highest
Rejoice and Be Glad

When the angels went away from them into heaven, the shepherds said to one another, "Let us go over to Bethlehem and see this thing that has happened, which the Lord has made known to us." **Luke 2:15**

Go and Tell

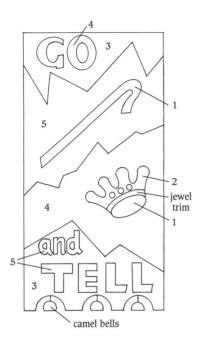

Suggested Colors

1–Dark brown

2–Deep gold

3–Emerald green

4–White

5–Yellow gold

Symbolism and Meaning

The season of Epiphany is the time when we move from the birth of Christ to the proclamation of the Good News of great joy to all people. The crown symbolizes Christ leaving the throne of heaven to become a Shepherd to the flock of humankind, represented by the shepherd's crook.

The faint tinkling sound of camel bells carries us back to the time of Christ's birth and reminds us of the travelers responding to the call to "go over to Bethlehem and see this thing that has happened."

Today we celebrate the season of Epiphany as we respond to the call to "Go and Tell." An appropriate hymn, which reinforces the Epiphany message is "Go Tell It on the Mountain."

Suggested Materials

Use medium weight fabric such as chino for green and white backgrounds. Taffeta or similar high sheen fabric can be used for the yellow background and the words "and Tell." Use a rough-textured fabric for the crook and the inside of the crown. Velveteen and pieces of jewelry or plastic gems can be used to decorate the crown. Camel bells can be purchased at discount, arts-and-crafts, or novelty stores and used to trim the bottom of the banner.

Worship the King

When they saw the star, they rejoiced exceedingly with great joy. And going into the house they saw the child with Mary His mother, and they fell down and worshiped Him. **Matthew 2:10–11**

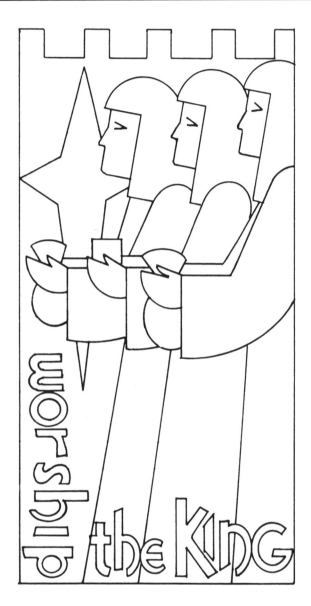

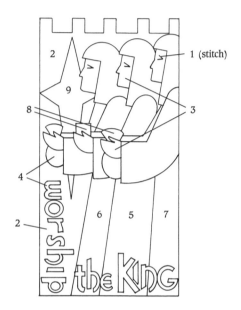

Suggested Colors

1–Black	6–Royal blue
2–Bright green	7–Royal purple
3–Flesh tone	8–Silver
4–Gold	9–White
5–Red	

Symbolism and Meaning

The star in the East that heralded Christ's birth shone brightly as it led the Magi to the Christ Child. In humble adoration for a king they scarcely understood, they fell down and worshiped Him with their gifts.

These first gifts freely brought to the Christ Child represent our natural response of adoration and worship to our loving King. The message of this Epiphany banner comes from the hymn, "Oh, Worship the King."

Suggested Materials

Use medium weight chino for the background. Lightly textured, flesh-toned fabric such as kettle cloth or linen is good for the faces and hands. Use black stitching for the eyes. Use satin or similar high sheen fabric for the star. Use gold lamé for the letters and bags of coins; silver lamé for the other gifts.

And He withdrew from them about a stone's throw, and knelt down and prayed, "Father, if Thou art willing, remove this cup from Me; nevertheless not My will, but Thine, be done." **Luke 22:41–42 RSV**

Thy Will Be Done

Suggested Colors

1–Blue red

2–Dark purple

3–Off-white

Symbolism and Meaning

In His state of humility in the Garden of Gethsemane, our Lord experienced the agony of His mission to rescue humanity. Although He fervently prayed that His cup of suffering would be removed, He obediently yielded to the will of the Father in accepting the degrading death He had to endure. "Not My Will but Thine" is our Lenten call to complete submission to God's will in our lives.

Suggested Materials

Use a textured drapery fabric for the background, broadcloth for the cup, and chino for the letters. You can also trim the banner with dark purple tassels.

Suggested Titles

Not My Will But Thine

Thy Will Be Done

Take Up Your Cross

And He said to all, "If anyone would come after Me, let him deny himself and take up his cross daily and follow Me. For whoever would save his life will lose it, but whoever loses his life for My sake will save it. For what does it profit a man if he gains the whole world and loses or forfeits himself?" **Luke 9:23–25**

Suggested Colors

1–Beige
2–Brown
3–Dark purple
4–Light gray
5–Light purple
6–Tan
7–White

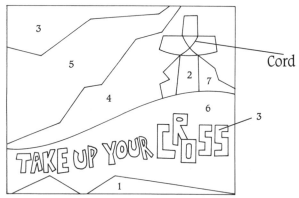

Symbolism and Meaning

The cross stands starkly outlined against a sky of darkness and gloom, its message of suffering and death hanging heavy on our hearts. A small light breaks forth from behind the cross.

It is an intense light that declares to us the message of self-denial and decision. As Jesus said, if we are to be His followers, we will surely take up crosses daily. When our crosses seem to hold disappointment or frustration, we look beyond the gloomy Good Friday cross to the victorious Easter hope. The light in our life shines as we deny self and acknowledge Christ as the authority in our lives. In this passage Jesus promises that by selflessly losing our life in service to Him, we will truly find it.

Suggested Materials

Use rough-textured fabrics for the cross and hill. Use medium weight fabric such as chino for the sky, letters, and white light behind the cross. Use cording for the cross binding.

And by that will we have been sanctified through the offering of the body of Jesus Christ once for all. **Hebrews 10:10**

Once for All

large nails

Suggested Colors

  1–Beige

  2–Brown

  3–Burgundy

  4–Dark brown

  5–Dark purple

  6–Light purple

Symbolism and Meaning

The cross is given the place of prominence in this banner. The crown of thorns, drops of blood, and large nails emphasize the role of Christ as the sacrificial Lamb, a substitute for the priestly sacrifices offered in the Hebrew temple to atone for the sins of the people.

Through this offering of His sinless body, He purchased a clean slate for humankind in the eyes of God, opening forever the doors of heaven to all who believe. The cross looms high above us, bidding us to look up and truly see what Christ has done for us.

Suggested Materials

Use rough-textured fabric for the cross and crown. Use medium weight fabric such as broadcloth for the background, letters, and drops of blood. Stitch the cross in a dark shade of purple. Add large nails or spikes to the bottom of the banner.

Hosanna!

And the crowds that went before Him and that followed Him were shouting, "Hosanna to the Son of David! Blessed is He who comes in the name of the Lord! Hosanna in the highest!" **Matthew 21:9**

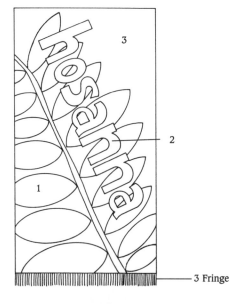

3 Fringe

Suggested Colors

1–Bright green

2–Red orange

3–White

Symbolism and Meaning

Imagine the excitement of this festive day—the road strewn with palm branches, the people waving them in the air and shouting, "Hosanna! Blessed is He who comes in the name of the Lord. Hosanna in the highest!" What a scene to have witnessed—the triumphal entry into Jerusalem of Jesus, the Son of David, in fulfillment of messianic prophecy!

Although we were not eyewitnesses to His triumphal entry into Jerusalem, we are witnesses to His triumphal entry into our lives each Sunday. On Palm Sunday we recall the beginning of the most dramatic week in all history. The triumphant hosannas preface the sober events of Holy Week with joy surpassed only by the shouts of "He is risen!" on Easter morning.

Suggested Materials

Use chino or dressy fabric for the background, palm branch, and letters. White fringe can be used for the trim at the bottom.

Suggested Titles

Hosanna
Hosanna in the Highest!

No Greater Love

Greater love has no one than this, that someone lays down his life for his friends.
John 15:13

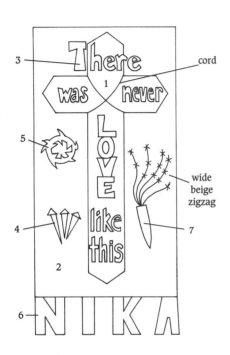

Suggested Colors

1–Beige	5–Light purple
2–Black	6–Off-white
3–Blue red	7–Tan
4–Gray	

Symbolism and Meaning

The solemn events of Good Friday are almost beyond our comprehension. To understand the humiliation Christ endured for us in the mockery of His trial, the unmerciful flogging, the taunting as King of the Jews, and His final sacrifice as He was brutally nailed to the cross, we speak in negative terms. The words to describe this love come haltingly and clumsily to our limited minds as we struggle to understand a love we do not deserve. Quietly we stand in awe on Good Friday as we humbly acknowledge that the world has never seen such great love.

Across the bottom of this banner hangs the Greek word NIKA, meaning victor, a reminder that even in the midst of the horrible events of this day, hope would dawn on Easter morning.

Suggested Materials

Use rough-textured fabric for the cross, crown, nails, and whip. Use a wide beige zigzag stitch to finish the whip. Use medium weight fabric such as broadcloth for the background and letters, and cording for the cross binding.

Suggested Titles

There Was Never Love Like This
No Greater Love

Risen Indeed

He is not here, for He has risen, as He said.
Come, see the place where He lay.
Matthew 28:6

colored
glass

Suggested Colors

1–Apple green

2–Kelly green

3–Orange

4–Orange red

5–White

6–Yellow

Symbolism and Meaning

Whatever reactions the events of Holy Week brought forth in the despairing disciples of that day or bring forth in doubting people of our time, the fact is boldly and forever inscribed on the heart of history—He won! Doubts are dispelled; gloom is erased; confidence is restored; victory is certain. Sin and death are defeated.

The sun appeared over the jagged peaks of the disciples' shattered dream, chasing away the pain of the past three days and in the warmth of its vibrant light restoring hope and announcing to the world that "Christ is risen indeed!" The diamond-shaped glass crystals reflect and magnify the light of this resurrection message.

Suggested Materials

Use chino for the hills, and medium to high sheen fabrics for the sun, sky, and letters. Hang diamond-shaped colored glass along the bottom of the banner.

> Therefore, if anyone is in Christ, he is a new creation. The old has passed away; behold, the new has come. **2 Corinthians 5:17**

We Are the New Creation

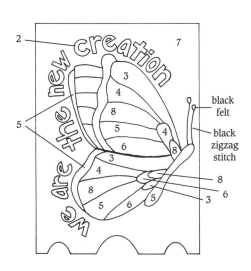

Suggested Colors

1–Black	5–Orange
2–Blue	6–Red
3–Bright blue	7–White
4–Green	8–Yellow

Symbolism and Meaning

The caterpillar reaches a stage in its limited, life when the former way is no longer adequate; it is almost as if it realizes that there is more. At that point, trusting nature to complete the cycle, it spins a cocoon in which the metamorphosis of giving up the former self to become a new creature occurs. As assuredly as the butterfly emerges from the cocoon a more beautiful and glorious version of the original creature, Christians, too, experience their own change as they shed their old nature and emerge in the new nature of Christ.

No longer content to spend its days groveling on the ground, the butterfly now flourishes in the freedom of making its contribution to God's creation. Likewise, new creatures in Christ confidently face their circumstances on wings of victory rather than in the bonds of defeat.

Suggested Materials

Use chino or other dressy fabric for the background. Medium to high sheen fabrics can be used for the letters and butterfly. The body and the edges of the wings are one piece of orange fabric stitched in contrasting thread. Use a black zigzag stitch and black felt for the antennae.

Suggested Titles

Created Anew
We Are the New Creation

Jesus Lives

But for you who revere My name, the sun of righteousness will rise with healing in its wings. And you will go out and leap like calves released from the stall. **Malachi 4:2**

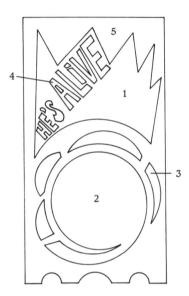

Suggested Colors
1–Bright yellow

2–Burnt orange

3–Orange

4–Royal blue

5–White

Symbolism and Meaning

Like the phoenix rising out of the ashes of the somber season of Lent, the light of Easter bursts forth on the horizon of humankind's dark despair, flooding the world with hope. The outstretched arms of the suffering Christ on the cross are triumphantly transformed into the buoyant arms of a Savior lifting us into the way, the truth, and the life.

"He's alive!" is the energizing cry that spawned Christianity and sustains Christians today. The burnt orange ball of fire represents Christ, the "Sun of righteousness" referred to in Scripture. The lighter orange rays, representing Christians in the world who reflect His love and light, emanate from Christ, the central source of power. The yellow sunburst explodes with the message that "He's alive!" and that we can in truth "go out and leap like calves released from the stall."

Suggested Materials

Use medium weight fabrics such as trigger, chino, or broadcloth in vivid colors. For a dressy effect, use high sheen fabrics for the symbols.

Suggested Titles

He's Alive

Jesus Lives

Leap for Joy!

And very early on the first day of the week, when the sun had risen, they went to the tomb. **Mark 16:2**

Morning Has Broken

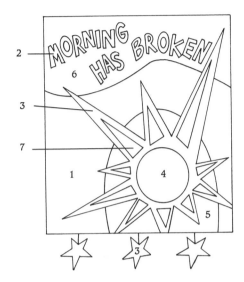

Suggested Colors

1–Beige

2–Bright sky blue

3–Orange

4–Red orange

5–Royal purple

6–White

7–Yellow

Symbolism and Meaning

When she arrived at the Lord's tomb, Mary was seized with despair and helplessness as she saw that it lay empty. Imagine Mary's desperation in the following moments as she unknowingly encountered Jesus. "Jesus said to her, 'Woman, why are you weeping? Who are you seeking?' Supposing Him to be the gardener, she said to Him, 'Sir, if You have carried Him away, tell me where You have laid Him, and I will take Him away.'" (John 20:15).

To the woman whose life had been irrevocably changed by the mercy and grace He taught, Jesus spoke tenderly, "Mary." She turned to the One who spoke, and her heart must have quickened with joy as she recognized our Lord. Filled with wonder and amazement at Him who stood before her, she responded, "Rabboni!"

Morning had broken for Mary Magdalene, just as it has for all who, by the power of the Holy Spirit, believe in the work of our Lord Jesus to bring forgiveness. To trust in His work is to trust in the reality of His payment for our sins, the victory of life over death and light over darkness. Christ's triumph shines forth brilliantly, shattering forever the death and darkness of the tomb.

Suggested Materials

Use chino for the sky and letters, rough-textured fabric for the tomb, broadcloth for the inside of the tomb, and high sheen fabric for the sunburst. The trim of three sunbursts should be high sheen satin, either sewn and stuffed or cut and glued to both sides of heavy cardboard.

Come, Holy Spirit

I baptize you with water for repentance, but He who is coming after me is mightier than I, whose sandals I am not worthy to carry. He will baptize you with the Holy Spirit and with fire. **Matthew 3:11**

Suggested Colors
1–Orange
2–Orange red
3–Red
4–White

Symbolism and Meaning

Mighty winds descended from heaven, and the fires of Pentecost came to rest on the heads of the astonished disciples, signaling the birth of the Christian Church. God's generous outpouring of His Spirit, which moved these people to share the Gospel of Jesus Christ with people of such diverse backgrounds and varied languages, demonstrates His willingness to share His Spirit with all who hear His call. The Holy Spirit penetrates and lives in Christians everywhere, manifesting Himself and calling to us through the Word and Sacraments. In response to His calling, the Church prays, "Come, Holy Spirit."

The shape of a dove, a Christian symbol for the Holy Spirit, is formed by the tongues of flame, representing the outpouring of God's Spirit on His people.

Suggested Materials

Use chino or medium sheen fabric for the background, flames, and dove. Use medium weight fabric such as broadcloth for the letters.

34

And in the last days it shall be, God declares, that I will pour out my Spirit upon all flesh.
Acts 2:17 RSV

Receive the Holy Spirit

Suggested Colors

1–Orange

2–Orange red

3–Red

4–Royal blue

5–White

Symbolism and Meaning

After Jesus' ascension, the disciples banded together, continually devoted themselves to prayer, and remained in Jerusalem until the Comforter was sent.

On the Day of Pentecost, their time of waiting abruptly ended with the sudden rush of a mighty wind from heaven. As the fires of Pentecost appeared above each of them, Peter, surging with the power of the promised Holy Spirit, hastened to interpret the supernatural events to the crowd. Raising his voice, he declared that this was not a drunken revelry at nine o'clock in the morning, but the fulfillment of the prophecy spoken by Joel that God's Spirit would be poured out on all flesh, as well as the fulfillment of the promise of Jesus that the Comforter would come.

The tongues of fire fell from heaven, the Spirit was poured forth with the rush of a mighty wind, and the Church was born as a living testimony to the love of God in Jesus Christ.

Suggested Materials

Use medium weight chino or other moderate sheen fabric for the flames and water. The background and letters can be any medium weight fabric.

Suggested Titles

I Will Pour Out My Spirit upon All Flesh
Receive the Holy Spirit

35

Three in One

The grace of the Lord Jesus Christ and the love of God and the fellowship of the Holy Spirit be with you all. **2 Corinthians 13:14**

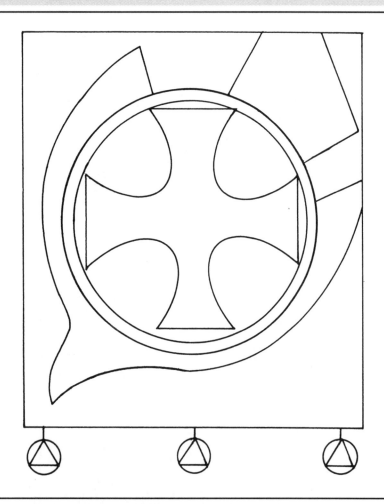

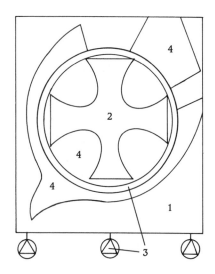

Suggested Colors

1–Beige

2–Emerald green

3–Gold

4–White

Symbolism and Meaning

At the heart of the Christian faith is the belief in a triune God who deliberately reveals Himself as God the Father, God the Son, and God the Holy Spirit. The three persons of the Trinity function together with special roles in one divine purpose:

God the Father is infinite in wisdom, power, and love and is the Maker and Ruler of all things, the Almighty, the great "I Am," who was and is and ever shall be. He is represented in the banner by the circle of the Alpha and Omega, the beginning and the end.

God the Son is God manifest in the flesh, Jesus Christ, bearing the burden of redeeming God's lost creation through His own death, thereby becoming the Savior of the world. He is represented in the banner by the symbol which has become synonymous with His name—the cross. The Father's love

encompassed in the Son is shown by the circle encompassing the cross.

God the Holy Spirit, symbolized by the dove, embodies the divine presence of God in our lives, through the Word of God. By means of the Holy Word, the Spirit guides, strengthens, and comforts us in time of need and perpetually reminding us of the truth of Christ.

The three triangles in circles represent the singular roles of each person of the Trinity, while the three symbols on the banner itself are superimposed, portraying the oneness of the three.

Suggested Materials

Use medium weight, high sheen fabrics such as satin, or use chino if less sheen is desired. Use gold lamé for the Trinity symbols across the bottom and the ring around the cross. Or the Trinity symbols can be done in macramé.

So now faith, hope, and love abide, these three; but the greatest of these is love. **1 Corinthians 13:13**

The Greatest Is Love

Suggested Colors

1–Beige

2–Green

3–White

Symbolism and Meaning

The marriage banner combines the selfless love of God, poetically described by Paul in 1 Corinthians, with the romantic love of husband and wife, represented by the heart.

God's love in the marriage is the glue that cements the relationship, allowing romantic love to flourish, while nurturing the greater agape love for each other. It is this latter love that seals the marriage in a covenant protected by God. When all other selfish love falls short, God's selfless love sustains and continuously pours life into the relationship designed for husband and wife.

Suggested Materials

Use chino for the background unless a dressier fabric is desired. Use a high sheen fabric such as satin for the letters and heart. Cut the heart out of beige and apply green letters to it. Hearts at the bottom of the banner should be the same green as used in the banner and should be sewn, turned, and lightly stuffed.

Suggested Titles

The Greatest of These Is Love

The Greatest Is Love

Two Become One

"For this reason a man shall leave his father and mother and be joined to his wife, and the two shall become one flesh." So they are no longer two but one flesh. **Mark 10:7–8 RSV**

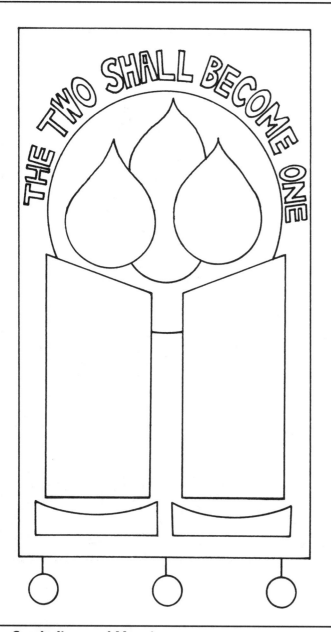

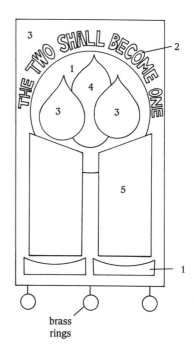

brass rings

Suggested Colors
1–Gold

2–Green

3–Ivory

4–Light camel

5–White

Symbolism and Meaning

The marriage banner portrays the union of two lives, blended in matrimony, becoming one with the Creator of that holy union.

The two distinct flames, representing the separate natures of man and woman, voluntarily fuse into the greater flame, signifying that the two have become one in Christ. The circle encompassing the flames represents the eternal nature of married love as ordained by God. The small rings across the bottom of the banner represent the outward sign of the inward love, the wedding ring.

Suggested Materials

Use gold lamé as specified and satin or other high sheen fabric for all other parts. Hang brass rings along the bottom.

Suggested Titles

The Two Shall Become One
Two Become One

Come to the Living Water

Whoever drinks of the water that I will give him will never be thirsty forever. The water that I will give him will become in him a spring of water welling up to eternal life. **John 4:14**

Suggested Colors

1–Bright blue

2–Bright green

3–White

Symbolism and Meaning

Parched and withered on the desert of life, seeking an oasis to quench the thirst and ease the scorched, burning dryness of a life off course—such is our situation when cut off from the Source of life.

"Come to the Living Water" is the invitation to the sacrament of Baptism for all who desire to drink the living water of Christ, which satisfies spiritual thirst and sustains life.

Suggested Materials

Use puff paint for the white portions of the pouring water and chino for the rest of the banner.

Create in Me a Clean Heart

Create in me a clean heart, O God,
and put a new and right spirit within me.
Psalm 51:10 RSV

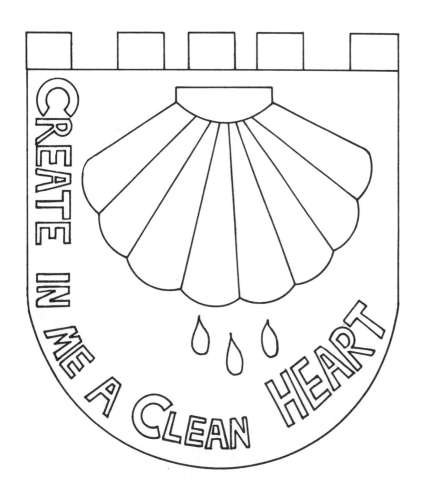

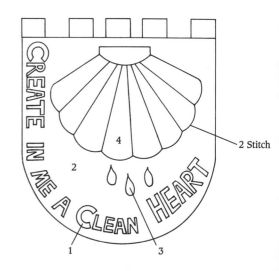

2 Stitch

Suggested Colors

1–Bright blue

2–Camel

3–Light blue

4–White

Symbolism and Meaning

Encumbered by his sinful nature and falling short of a right relationship with God, man is alienated from his Creator. From the time of the psalmist until today, man has sought release from his bondage and the renewal of a right spirit within through the cleansing of his heart. In Holy Baptism, restoration of harmony and purification of the heart occur through the cleansing power of God's grace. Washed clean by water and the Spirit, we stand before God clothed in the righteousness of Christ.

The cleansing drops of God's grace fall from the shell, a Christian symbol for Baptism.

Suggested Materials

Use medium sheen fabric such as chino for the entire banner. The shell is stark white stitched in camel.

And He took bread, and when He had given thanks, He broke it and gave it to them, saying, "This is My body, which is given for you. Do this in remembrance of Me." And likewise the cup after they had eaten, saying, "This cup that is poured out for you is the new covenant in My blood." **Luke 22:19–20**

Take, Eat, Drink, Remember

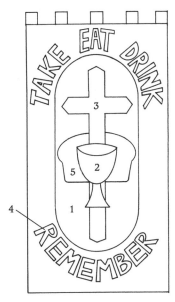

Suggested Colors

1–Beige

2–Blue gray

3–Brown

4–Burgundy

5–Camel

Symbolism and Meaning

Reclining around the table as was customary for the Passover meal, Jesus' disciples must have had strange reactions as He took the Passover bread and wine and, in complete departure from the customary ceremony, spoke the words of institution:

This is My body, broken for you—remember Me when you eat it. This is My blood, poured out for you—I am instituting today a new covenant with you—as often as you drink the wine, remember Me.

It is so natural for us, as we receive Holy Communion, to see the cross and remember that Christ died for our sins. For the disciples, however, confused by the meaning of His mysterious actions during the Passover meal, the cross was not yet a reality. One can only imagine their amazement as the realization of what He had done became clear to them.

Acting out the drama of the Last Supper in our minds takes us back to the scene in that upper room and vividly inscribes it on our hearts, compelling us each time we "take, eat, and drink" the elements of His new covenant to "remember."

Suggested Materials

Use medium weight fabric such as chino, broadcloth, or trigger.

Suggested Titles

Take, Eat, Drink, Remember

Partake and Remember

Come to the Table

Now as they were eating, Jesus took bread, and after blessing it broke it and gave it to the disciples, and said, "Take, eat; this is My body." And He took a cup, and when He had given thanks He gave it to them, saying, "Drink of it, all of you, for this is My blood of the covenant, which is poured out for many for the forgiveness of sins." **Matthew 26:26–28**

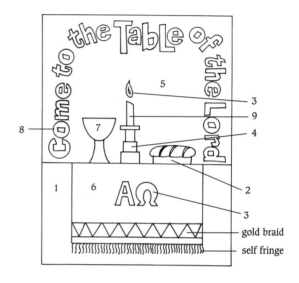

Suggested Colors

1–Brown	6–Off-white
2–Camel	7–Pewter
3–Gold	8–Red
4–Light brown	9–White
5–Light violet	

Symbolism and Meaning

As the good Host welcoming His guests to the lavish feast, our Lord invites us to the incomparable feast of Holy Communion. The table awaits the presence of the Host manifested in the elements of bread and wine, Christ's very body and blood broken and poured out for us.

Completely aware of our own sin and unworthiness, we come humbly seeking and gratefully accepting His generous pardon. Forgiven, loved, and free, we depart, having shared in the Meal, which continues to sustain long after the gathering is over.

Suggested Materials

Use medium weight fabric such as broadcloth for all items except the candlestick, the table (which should resemble wood as nearly as possible), and the cloth covering the table (which should be white wool with a two-inch fringe at the bottom). The coarser fabrics are used to represent folk worship. Use a wooden rod and wooden drapery rings to hang the banner, and gold braid to decorate the bottom of the tablecloth.

Suggested Titles

Come to the Table of the Lord
Come to the Table

For whoever would save his life will lose it, but whoever loses his life for My sake and the gospel's will save it. **Mark 8:35**

Take My Life

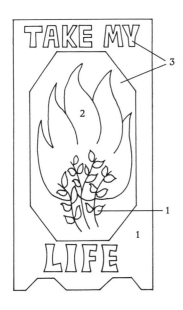

Suggested Colors

1–Green

2–Red orange

3–White

Symbolism and Meaning

Moses heard God's call in the commanding presence of the burning bush. God wanted him, but Moses hesitated. God had a purpose for Moses, but Moses doubted his ability to function as God's messenger and the leader of His people. God wanted Moses to surrender his life, but Moses was unwilling to trust God.

God's call to yield our lives to Him, although not always as dramatic as His call to Moses, clearly pierces the stillness of our minds. Many have heard it; some have replied. When we see ourselves as Moses saw himself—unworthy and unable—we selfishly cling to a life that is not rightly ours, doubting that with God all things are possible. Only when we are enabled by His grace, through the water and Word of Holy Baptism, to surrender our lives to the Creator to be used for His purposes can we experience abundant living.

As He releases His power in us, we leave hesitation, doubt, and unwillingness behind, no longer seeking to gain the whole world and in the process actually forfeiting our own lives.

Moses' ultimate decision to respond with "Take my life" expresses the significance of the confirmation commitment as we offer our best to the Lord.

Suggested Materials

Use chino or other medium sheen fabric for the flame and the bush. Use medium weight fabric such as broadcloth or trigger for the rest of the banner.

Firm in Your Faith

Be watchful, stand firm in the faith,
act like men, be strong.

1 Corinthians 16:13

Suggested Colors
1–Gold
2–Green
3–White

Symbolism and Meaning

A voyager floats aimlessly in an immense sea, waves of uncertainty, temptation, and loneliness lapping against his craft, each one pulling him perilously close to the edge. Lost at sea, adrift with no purposeful direction, he desperately searches for an anchor that will secure his position.

The anchor of stability we all seek is the faith we boldly affirm in the act of confirmation, a faith that securely ties us to the Father through the death and resurrection of Jesus Christ by the power of the Holy Spirit. It is not enough to let the anchor of faith down only part way into the dark waters of life. We must fully extend it, although we often do not see its intended course, until it is firmly grounded in our sure foundation, Jesus Christ.

Suggested Materials

Use medium weight fabrics such as chino or broadcloth. For a more dressy effect use a high sheen fabric for the anchor.

Suggested Titles

Firm in Your Faith
Stand Firm

With Him in Paradise

And he said, "Jesus, remember me when You come into Your kingdom." And He said to him, "Truly, I say to you, today you will be with Me in Paradise." Luke 23:42–43

Suggested Colors

1–Apple green	7–Medium gray
2–Bright blue	8–Peach
3–Charcoal gray	9–Pink
4–Dark peach	10–White
5–Emerald green	11–Yellow
6–Light gray	

Symbolism and Meaning

The death of a loved one calls forth, perhaps more than any other life-changing event, a myriad of conflicting emotions in those who must live with the absence of a dear and familiar face. Grasping for any and every means of solace to alleviate the burden of sorrow, a turn toward the One who conquered death itself is often the soothing balm that comforts the mourner.

Remembering Jesus' comforting words of assurance to the thief on the cross who came to know the Savior during the last moments of his life, brings a quiet peace to the hearts of the grief-stricken mourners. His promise that "today you will be with Me in Paradise" assures all believers of an eternal place with Him. The water and the Word remind us of the gifts of the Holy Baptism—forgiveness and the promise of eternal life—that bring a ray of hope amid the shadow of sorrow.

The peace of the river in the midst of the "valley of death" and the sun shining from beneath the clouds speak for themselves in this funeral banner.

Suggested Materials

Use any medium weight, medium tone fabric for the sun and rays. Use medium weight, light texture fabric for the clouds and a medium weight fabric such as trigger for the hills and river. Make the letters and the sun the same dark peach.

Suggested Titles

With Him in Paradise
Today You Will Be with Me in Paradise

A Place Prepared

And if I go and prepare a place for you,
I will come again and will take you to
Myself, that where I am you may be also.
John 14:3

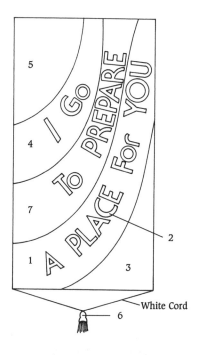

White Cord

Suggested Colors

1–Blue	5–Pink
2–Bright green	6–White
3–Green	7–Yellow
4–Peach	

Symbolism and Meaning

When Jesus ascended and left His followers to live in the world without Him, they must have experienced to some extent the feeling of helplessness and loss that invades the heart of a grieving person in the early hours of adjustment to life without a loved one.

Faith in His promise to go and prepare a place for us and to come and receive us into that place plants hope in the midst of despair and trust that there is life beyond death, a permanent home with the Lord and with the loved ones who have gone before. We express this faith when we confess our belief "in the resurrection of the dead and the life of the world to come."

The upward sweep of Jesus' ascension promise reminds us that in Him we move beyond death to eternal life.

Suggested Materials

Use any medium weight fabric in pastel tones for all parts of the banner except the letters, which should be bright green. Use a narrow white satin cord to hang the tassel. A quarter-inch dowel rod inserted in a casing across the bottom will allow the tassel and cord to hang properly.

Suggested Titles

I Go to Prepare a Place for You
A Place Prepared

Honor the LORD with your wealth and
with the firstfruits of all your produce.

Proverbs 3:9

What Can I Give?

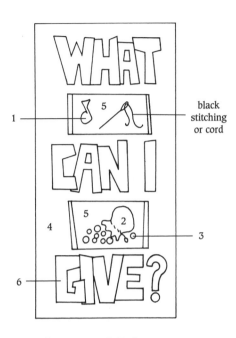

black
stitching
or cord

Suggested Colors

1–Black

2–Gold

3–Silver

4–Turquoise

5–White

6–Yellow

Symbolism and Meaning

Each new morning offers us the opportunity to make our day the Lord's day by asking Him "What can I give You today, Lord?"

We wonder: Will it be my time given to someone in need or to a demanding task; my talent given in teaching a class, serving on a committee or board, or witnessing to a brother or sister; or my material possessions given to alleviate another's poverty or to support the work of those who penetrate the world with the Good News?

Turning to the Source of unconditional giving, we ask for open eyes to see the needs around us and to look for ways to respond, for ears to hear His call to tasks that further His purpose, for energy to rise to those occasions when we are asked to use our talents, and for hearts to generously support the work of His kingdom on earth with the best of the time, talents, and possessions He has so freely given.

Suggested Materials

Use medium weight fabrics such as broadcloth or trigger and silver lamé where specified. Use black stitching or cord to create the thread in the needle.

Teach Me, Lord

Teach me, O LORD, the way of Your statutes; and I will keep it to the end. Give me understanding, that I may keep Your law and observe it with my whole heart. **Psalm 119:33–34**

Suggested Colors

1–Fuchsia

2–Gold

3–Ivory

4–Light gray

5–White

6–Yellow orange

Symbolism and Meaning

The Holy Spirit beckons us to the pages of the open Bible, pages filled with the knowledge of God's heart, His revelation of the key to the abundant life. To turn away from the Scriptures after accepting Christ as Lord is to cast a shadow of darkness over our spiritual growth. To turn to Him and implore, "Teach me, Lord," is to ask Him to unlock the hidden treasures of His Word and fill the open vessel of our hearts and minds with His message.

Illuminating the entire banner is the light of truth, representing the Holy Spirit, who clarifies mysteries, imparts knowledge, and conveys truth. Guided through the Scriptures by His unerring instruction, we have access to God's wisdom and are freed from the hindrance of our limited comprehension. The lamp of knowledge liberally shines on our understanding as we come to truly know the Lord.

Suggested Materials

Use medium fabric for all parts of banner—chino, broadcloth, or trigger. Use ivory material outlined with black stitches and flat gold cord for the pages.

Praise the LORD, for the LORD is good; sing to His name, for it is pleasant! **Psalm 135:3**

Praise Him

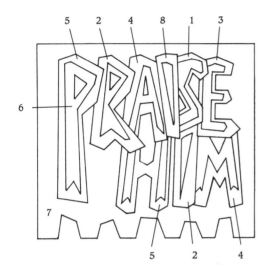

Suggested Colors

1–Blue	5–Red
2–Green	6–Silver
3–Orange	7–White
4–Purple	8–Yellow

Symbolism and Meaning

The Scriptures are laced with praise. They extol it as a vehicle of communication to exalt, applaud, acclaim, and glorify our Creator, Deliverer, Fortress, Shield, and Stronghold, to use some of the words of the psalmist.

The nature of praise is ingrained in the many expressions of worship, although praise is not confined to the formal worship service. Desiring and seeking our continual praise, whether that is in our spontaneous daily songs of thanksgiving or in the Gloria Patri of the gathered congregation, God fills our praise with His presence.

Psalm 150 exhorts all living creatures to praise their Maker:

Praise Him with the sounding of the trumpet, praise Him with the harp and lyre, praise Him with tambourine and dancing, praise Him with the strings and flute, praise Him with the clash of cymbals, praise Him with resounding cymbals. Let everything that has breath praise the LORD! Praise the LORD! (3–6)

Suggested Materials

Use satin, taffeta, or other high sheen fabric for the letters and silver lamé for the overlays. Use chino or medium weight moderate sheen for the background.

We Adore Thee

Oh come, let us sing to the LORD; let us make a joyful noise to the rock of our salvation!

Psalm 95:1

Suggested Colors

1–Black

2–Gold

3–Light tan

4–Royal blue

5–White

Symbolism and Meaning

"Joyful, Joyful, We Adore Thee," the powerful hymn in which Henry Van Dyke's poem is set to the music of Beethoven's Ninth Symphony, infuses this banner with its compelling strains of magnificent gladness. Any reference to this beautiful "Ode to Joy" would be incomplete without the words of the hymn itself.

Our hearts do indeed unfold like flowers before the God of glory in the singing of this song of gladness, as we embrace the Lord of love, who dispels the clouds of sin and sadness from our lives, replacing them with immortal gladness. The wellspring of the joy of living lifts us to the joy divine, leading us sunward in the triumphant song of life.

Suggested Materials

Use chino or moderate sheen fabric for the background and music staff. The music staff should be outlined in black stitching. Glue on narrow black satin cord for the lines of the staff, the outline of the note, and the treble clef. Use black felt for music notes. Use gold lamé for the trumpet and satin or another high sheen fabric for the letters. Insert brass rods at the top and bottom.

Suggested Titles

Joyful, Joyful, We Adore Thee
We Adore Thee

He said to him the third time, "Simon, son of John, do you love Me?" Peter was grieved because He said to him the third time, "Do you love Me?" and he said to Him, "Lord, You know everything; You know that I love You." Jesus said to him, "Feed My sheep." **John 21:17**

Feed My Sheep

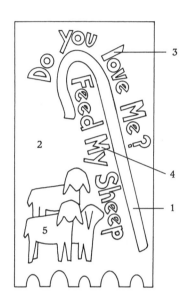

Suggested Colors

1–Brown

2–Green

3–Orange

4–Red orange

5–White

Symbolism and Meaning

Breakfast was over. Jesus turned to Peter and asked him an unusual question: "Simon, son of John, do you love Me more than these?" Peter was quick to respond, "Yes, Lord; You know that I love You." Jesus told him to feed His lambs. A second time Jesus said to him, "Simon, son of John, do you love Me?" Again Peter replied, "Yes, Lord; You know that I love You." And Jesus told him to take care of His sheep. When Jesus asked him a third time, "Simon, son of John, do you love Me?" Peter, grieved that the Lord should be so uncertain of his devotion, replied, "Lord, You know everything; You know that I love You." Jesus said again, "Feed My sheep" (John 21:15–17).

Yes, He was talking about people, not sheep, and He was talking not only to Peter. The pilgrimage of faith eventually leads us to the same conclusion that Peter ultimately reached by the power of the Holy Spirit: Love of God is not an end in itself; it is the inspiration that compels us to a life of feeding others with the daily bread of the Good Shepherd and with the bread and wine of Holy Communion.

Suggested Materials

Use medium weight fabrics such as trigger or broadcloth for the background, words, and shepherd's crook. Use textured wool for the sheep.

Suggested Titles

Love Feeds Others
Do You Love Me? Feed My Sheep
Feed My Sheep

Fishers of Men

Jesus said to them, "Follow Me, and I will make you become fishers of men." **Mark 1:17**

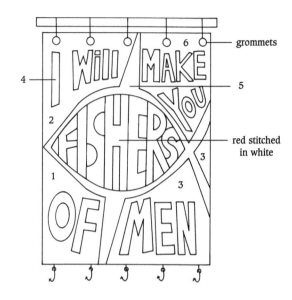

grommets

red stitched in white

Suggested Colors
1–Bright blue
2–Bright green
3–Purple
4–Red
5–White
6–Yellow

Symbolism and Meaning

"Follow Me," He said, "and I will make you fishers of men." Laying down their nets, without looking back, the men of the sea turned to follow in the footsteps of the great Fisherman. Be it a walk along the shores of Galilee or into the hearts of others, they were ready, knowing somehow that they could entrust their very lives to Him.

Using the well-developed skills of their forsaken trade, now transformed by Jesus into skills they would use to cast out the nets of the Gospel, the hardy fishermen became "Fishers of Men." The simple command beckons us as invitingly now as it did then: "Follow Me. I will take you as you are and make you what you can be, and through you

My nets will be cast into the world."

It would be appropriate to sing the hymn "Fishers of Men" in conjunction with the hanging of this banner.

Suggested Materials

Use trigger or broadcloth, whichever produces a more vivid color. Outline the red letters of the word "fishers" in white stitching. A wooden rod, rope, grommets, and large gold fishhooks are needed to complete the banner.

Suggested Titles

I Will Make You Fishers of Men
Fishers of Men

For by grace you have been saved through faith. And this is not your own doing; it is the gift of God. **Ephesians 2:8**

Saved by Grace

Suggested Colors
1–Black
2–Green
3–Red
4–White
5–Yellow
6–Yellow orange

Symbolism and Meaning

His heart filled with doubt concerning church procedures, especially the practice of purchasing indulgences to buy the soul's way into heaven, Luther nailed his 95 theses to the chapel door at the University of Wittenberg. The Protestant Reformation, fueled by Paul's writings on grace, had been ignited.

Luther's beliefs and his bold fervor in the face of mighty odds continue to fire our own faith. We cannot purchase, earn, or will salvation for ourselves; to claim otherwise is to remove the power of Christ's death and resurrection. We are saved by God's freely given grace, a gift we can receive only through faith in Jesus Christ. For Luther, as well as for all believers, it is the realization of God's generous outpouring of grace in our lives that brings us to faith and carries us into action. The banner depicts God's loving gift of grace received by us through faith in our Savior. The heart, cross, and light call to mind Luther's emblem.

Suggested Materials

Use medium weight fabrics such as chino, broadcloth, or trigger in vivid colors. Attach green fringe to the bottom of the banner.

With Him Forever

And I shall dwell in the house of the LORD forever. **Psalm 23:6 RSV**

Suggested Colors

1–Light gray

2–Navy

3–White

4–Yellow

Symbolism and Meaning

All Saints' Day is when we celebrate all the baptized, both those at rest and those still laboring on earth. It is a celebration of God's gifts to His people in Holy Baptism. And on All Souls Day we pause to remember the faithful departed, those godly persons who, in the living of their lives, indelibly engraved on our hearts a lasting influence. Guided by their examples and encouraged by their faith, we offer thanksgiving to God for their lives and rest in the assurance of the joy pervading their eternal existence around His throne.

Suggested Materials

Use a high sheen fabric for the stars and a heavy weight fabric for the cross and letters. You may need to use double fabric and fusible interface to prevent the navy background from showing through. Use medium weight fabric for the background and steeple. The entire steeple should be outline-stitched in a dark contrasting color. Attach yellow fringe to the bottom of the banner.

Suggested Titles

With Him Forever

I Shall Dwell in the House of the Lord Forever

> Lo, I am with you Always, even unto the end of the world. Amen.
> **Matthew 28:20 KJV**

With You Always

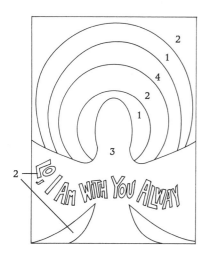

Suggested Colors
1–Blue
2–Green
3–White
4–Yellow

Symbolism and Meaning

In awe and silence on the Mount of Olives the disciples watched their beloved Master crown His earthly ministry by ascending to His heavenly home at the right hand of the Father's throne.

Feeling bereft of His guiding force in their lives, yet clinging to the memory of the strength He had provided, the laughter they had shared, and the knowledge He had imparted, the disciples feared that with His departure their faith would waver and their unity of purpose would be destroyed. Only His comforting words, "Lo, I am with you Always," gave them the confidence to continue. They trusted His promise to send the Spirit of truth, who would fill them with the power to persevere in their faith and go into all the world preaching the Good News and baptizing the nations in the name of the Triune God.

Suggested Materials

Use medium weight fabrics such as chino, broadcloth, or trigger in vivid colors.

Suggested Titles

With You Always
Lo, I Am with You Alway

Put on Christ

But put on the Lord Jesus Christ,
and make no provision for the flesh,
to gratify its desires. **Romans 13:14**

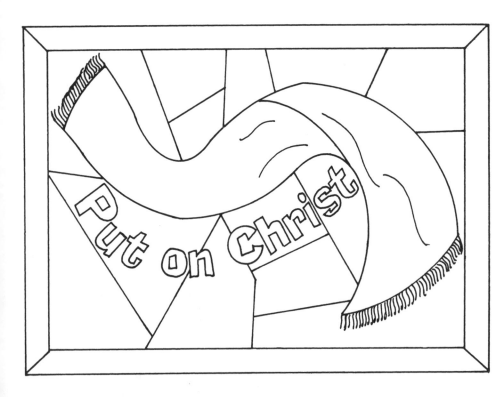

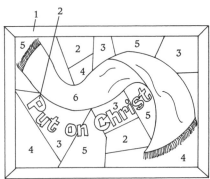

Suggested Colors
1–Black
2–Gold
3–Green
4–Red
5–Royal blue
6–White

Symbolism and Meaning

To put on something means to dress oneself in it, to make it part of one's behavior or appearance. For the Christian, putting on Christ involves discarding the old garment of self and replacing it with Christ's garment of compassion, kindness, humility, gentleness, patience, and forgiveness (Colossians 3:12–13).

This metaphor is difficult to understand outside of Christianity; it must be experienced from the inside. While the rest of the world bids us march to the hollow drumbeat of self-interest, Christ calls us to play in the symphony of selfless love.

A life alive in Christ and dead to self does not suffer an identity crisis, losing the entire personality and everything held dear. On the contrary, the new person, clothed in Christ, retains his distinctive characteristics, now refined and embellished by the touch of Christ, for new purposes. Daily, we are washed in the waters of Holy Baptism and, by the power of the Holy Spirit, we wear Christ's garments of righteousness and salvation.

The stole in this banner reminds us that as we arise each morning and dress in the garments that clothe our bodies, we clothe our minds in Him as we "put on Christ."

Suggested Materials

Use satin or high sheen fabric for the letters and background, which should look like stained glass. Use white wool for the stole with two-inch fringe at each end as shown. Use heavy, durable fabric for a black window frame. Stitch black lines between each section for a stained glass effect.

Raise a Banner

Lift ye up a banner upon the high mountain. **Isaiah 13:2 RSV**

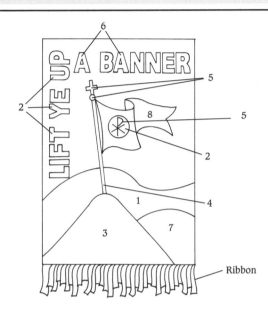

Suggested Colors

1–Beige	5–Gold
2–Bright royal blue	6–Light blue
3–Camel	7–Light camel
4–Dark brown	8–White

Symbolism and Meaning

Throughout history, banners have been prominently lifted to signal the imminence of important events—by rulers to claim dominion, by armies as a rallying point in battle, by proponents of a cause to declare a message, by nations as symbols embodying the principles they represent, and by religions to express beliefs.

Proudly, as children of the heavenly Father, we lift His royal banner on the high mountain, acknowledging His dominion, claiming His forgiveness, waving His message of love, and rallying people of all nations to the foot of the cross where love, mercy, and grace are freely given to all who acknowledge His lordship.

The banner of the Lord bears the emblem of the Chi-Rho within a circle, representing Christ in eternity, with the cross atop the standard proclaiming victory. The streamers across the bottom of the banner portray joy and freedom—rewards of allegiance to the heavenly King.

Suggested Materials

Use medium weight fabric with a rough texture such as suede cloth, no-wale corduroy, or linen-type drapery for the mountains. Use gold lamé for the Chi-Rho and cross with sphere. Use chino for the banner and medium weight trigger for everything else. Outline the banner on the hill in royal blue stitching. Attach varying lengths (5–8 inches) of one-inch grosgrain ribbon in alternating colors of the banner along the bottom. Use as many banner colors as possible (with exception of gold lamé) in the streamers. Use a wooden rod to hang. This banner would give a bolder effect in bright primary colors of red, yellow, and blue with green and white.

Suggested Titles

Lift Ye Up a Banner
Raise a Banner